The Ulti
Unofficial
Manchester
United Quiz Book

601 Fun Questions for United
Fans Everywhere

By
David Lynam

For Manchester United fans everywhere...

"The high point of my career was winning the Champions League. No one will ever erase that from my memory, in the same way that no one will ever erase the fact that I did it in a Manchester United shirt" - Cristiano Ronaldo

"It doesn't matter who leaves, the name of Manchester United does not leave" - Sir Alex Ferguson

"Man Utd,...they're still the best club on the planet, they've got the best supporters..." - Roy Keane

"I found the support inside Old Trafford has been terrific and, if there was ever a show of support for the football club and team, it was in this game. Inside Old Trafford it was really terrific, it really was" - David Moyes

# # #

Welcome to the ultimate Manchester United quiz book.

In this book you are going to find 601 questions about United, split into thirty separate rounds. You have the chance to test your knowledge and memory, and the questions cover a wide range of topics, including key matches, big transfers, past and present players, club history, and managers of the red devils.

The rounds are not split into themes, meaning that each round provides a random mix of trivia to test your knowledge. There is also a mix of difficulty, so this book will really test how much of a United buff you actually are. The book is interesting and informative, and will provide hours of fun for the most passionate United fans everywhere.

Good luck...

Table of Contents

# # #

Round 1:

1. Who scored the first goal in Manchester United's 2019-2020 home encounter with Arsenal in the Premier League?

2. Sir Alex Ferguson was appointed manager of Manchester United in 1986 after his predecessor was fired. Who was this predecessor?

3. Which team did Manchester United beat in the quarter final, on their way to winning the European Champions League in 1999?

4. Between the 2008-2009 and 2011-2012 seasons he averaged one hat-trick per season as a Manchester United player; but three of his four hat-tricks were scored in one season. Who was this player?

5. In the 2009-2010 Premier League season, Manchester United finished second in the league table. Who finished first?

6. Which Manchester United player retired with a career total of 129 international caps for Denmark?

7. Which Manchester United player was bailed until February 2008 after being arrested in December 2007?

8. Sir Alex Ferguson's first club signing was Viv Anderson. Which club was he brought from?

9. When was Manchester United founded?

10. Who lost to Manchester United in the 1991 final of the now defunct European Cup-Winners Cup?

11. At which stadium do Manchester United play their home games?

12. What was the score against Southampton at home on the 22 December 2001?

13. In which city was Ryan Giggs born?

14. 1964-65: Manchester United played Arsenal at Old Trafford. If United won this game they would win the championship with a game in hand. What was the final scoreline?

15. During the 1991 European Cup winner's cup success, Manchester United played one team from the English league during the campaign. Who were they?

16. What is the name of the trialist defender who made a couple of appearances for Manchester United in the 1995-96 season, includ22ing the 4-1 defeat on New Year's day to Tottenham Hotspur?

17. What is Mark Hughes' nickname?

18. Where did Manchester United sign Ruud Van Nistelrooy from?

19. Which club was Jesper Blomqvist signed from?

20. In the 1994 FA Cup Semi-Final replay against Oldham Athletic which Manchester United won 4-1, who scored United's first goal?

Answers:

1. Scott McTominay

2. Ron Atkinson

3. Inter Milan

4. Dimitar Berbatov

5. Chelsea

6. Peter Schmeichel

7. Jonny Evans

8. Arsenal

9. 1878

10. Barcelona

11. Old Trafford

12. 6-1

13. Cardiff

14. Manchester United 3 -1 Arsenal

15. Wrexham

16. William Prunier

17. Sparky

18. PSV Eindhoven

19. Parma

20. Denis Irwin

# # #

Round 2:

1. Who scored Manchester United's first goal in the 1968 European Cup Final?

2. Against whom did Andy Cole score his first league goal at Old Trafford?

3. In what year did Manchester United first win the European Cup?

4. When did Manchester United first win the F.A. Cup?

5. Which player, who had previously played under Sir Alex Ferguson at Aberdeen, was reunited with his old manager at Manchester United?

6. What club did Manchester United buy Antonio Valencia from?

7. This former Manchester United player had a very successful stay at the club, wearing the famous number 7 but scored only one hat-trick, which was against Newcastle United. Name the player.

8. On the 10th February 2008, when Manchester United honoured the lives lost in the Munich Air Disaster, the team's match shirts were designed like those back when the disaster happened on 6th February 1958. Who were Manchester United playing?

9. Who took Manchester United to the top of the pop charts in 1994 with, "Come on You Reds"?

10. Which Manchester United player kung fu kicked a Crystal Palace fan in January 1995?

11. Who did Sir Alex Ferguson sign for the club from Celtic in

1987?

12. When was the Manchester United Ladies FC founded?

13. Which Manchester United player was named English Footballer of the Year and PFA Player of the Year in 2000?

14. Who set the Manchester United goal scoring record in the 1970s?

15. Who were Manchester United playing when Nicky Butt was dismissed for the first time in senior competition, in January 1996?

16. In April 1992, Manchester United travelled to Liverpool knowing they had to win to stay in contention for the title. They lost 2-0. Who scored the Liverpool goals?

17. Manchester United had gone 40 years without defeat in European competition at home but this run was ended in the 1996-97 tournament. Which team ended that run?

18. The match immediately after Sir Matt Busby's death in 1994 was a home tie against Everton, which Manchester United won 1-0. Who scored the winning goal?

19. Who was given the nickname 'Seba'?

20. Where did Manchester United sign Steve Bruce from?

Answers:

1. Bobby Charlton

2. Manchester United

3. 1968

4. 1909

5. Gordon Strachan

6. Wigan Athletic

7. Cristiano Ronaldo

8. Manchester City

9. Status Quo

10. Eric Cantona

11. Brian McClair

12. 1977

13. Roy Keane

14. Bobby Charlton

15. West Ham United

16. Ian Rush & Mark Walters

17. Fenerbahce

18. Ryan Giggs

19. Juan Sebastian Veron

20. Norwich City

# # #

Round 3:

1. Who was the Manchester United manager when Sir Bobby Charlton ended his Old Trafford career?

2. Which team did Manchester United beat to reach the 1990 FA Cup Final?

3. From which team did Manchester United buy Alex Stepney?

4. Brian McClair scored the fourth goal in 1994 F.A.Cup defeat of Chelsea, but who set it up?

5. Who did Manchester United beat in the final, to win their first European Cup?

6. What year did Sir Alex Ferguson take over as manager?

7. Before suffering a double stress fracture in his back during the 2019-2020 season, which player led the charge as Manchester United's top goalscorer?

8. Who scored the winning goal for Manchester United in the second leg of the 1999 Champions League semi final against Juventus?

9. Which two legends have scored more than ten hat-tricks each for Manchester United?

10. When Bobby Charlton was honoured by Queen Elizabeth II for his services to football, he was given what title?

11. After the 2006 World Cup, how many different Manchester United players in their past had scored World Cup goals?

12. Which manager was sacked after a blaze of publicity after it was discovered he was having an extra-marital affair with

Manchester United physiotherapist Laurie Brown in July 1977?

13. From which coastal club was Lee Sharpe signed from?

14. What is the name of Manchester United's home ground?

15. Which club signed Paul Ince from Manchester United in 1995?

16. When Manchester United won the Premiership in 2002-2003 it was their which premiership title?

17. Who clinched the title for Arsenal at Old Trafford in the 2001/2002 season?

18. On which ground did Paul Scholes make his first team debut in November 1994?

19. Manchester United achieved their first League title success in 26 years in the 1992/1993 season. Which former Manchester United manager was the manager of the team which were runners-up that season?

20. In the 1994-1995 season, Manchester United travelled to Sweden to take on IFK Gothenburg in the Champions League group stage. They were beaten 3-1. Name the Gothenburg scorer who would later play for Manchester United?

Answers:

1. Tommy Docherty

2. Oldham Athletic

3. Chelsea

4. Paul Ince

5. Benfica

6. 1986

7. Marcus Rashford

8. Andy Cole

9. Denis Law and Jack Rowley

10. Sir Bobby Charlton

11. 18

12. Tommy Docherty

13. Torquay United

14. Old Trafford

15. Inter Milan

16. Eighth

17. Sylvain Wiltord

18. Vale Park

19. Ron Atkinson

20. Jesper Blomqvist

# # #

Round 4:

1. What was Bryan Robson's nickname?

2. Where did Manchester United sign Ray Wilkins from?

3. Which club did Frank O'Farrell leave to become Manchester United manager?

4. In the 1990 FA Cup Final against Crystal Palace the first game ended in a 3-3 draw. Who scored Manchester United's first goal?

5. After winning the European Cup in 1968, who did Manchester United play in the World Club Championship the following year?

6. Against whom did Ole Gunnar Solkjaer score his first league goal at Old Trafford?

7. Who did Sir Alex Ferguson succeed as manager?

8. Which Manchester United manager signed Bryan Robson?

9. What were the results of the two Manchester derbies in the Premier League in season 2019/2020? (United on the left, City on the right).

10. Following the 1990 FA Cup win, Manchester United qualified for the UEFA Cup Winners' Cup in the 1990-1991 season, which they would go on to win. Which team did they beat in the final?

11. How many matches did Manchester United lose on their way to clinching the Premier League in 1999?

12. Wayne Rooney scored a hat-trick on his Manchester United debut, which was a Champions League match. Which other player scored a hat-trick on his Manchester United debut?

13. When Manchester United won the UEFA Champions League

in 2008, it was their which European title?

14. Who scored the first Premiership goal at Old Trafford?

15. Which player admitted in his autobiography that he intended to hurt Alf-Inge Haland in a knee-high foul, which saw him sent off during a match against Manchester City in 2001?

16. From which club was Irish international Denis Irwin signed from?

17. Who was the first Manchester United captain who was from outside the United Kingdom or the Republic of Ireland?

18. Which Dutch player's transfer to Manchester United fell through after he failed a medical in 2000?

19. Who became Manchester United's record signing in 2002?

20. How many league goals did Ruud van Nistelrooy score during the 2001/2002 season?

Answers:

1. Captain marvel
2. Chelsea
3. Leicester City
4. Bryan Robson
5. Estudiantes
6. Blackburn Rovers
7. Ron Atkinson
8. Ron Atkinson
9. 2-1 away, 2-0 home
10. Barcelona
11. 3
12. Charles Sagar
13. Third
14. Peter Beardsley
15. Roy Keane
16. Oldham Athletic
17. Eric Cantona
18. Ruud van Nistelrooy
19. Rio Ferdinand
20. 23

# # #

Round 5:

1. Where in the table, did Manchester United finish in Sir Alex Ferguson's first full season south of the border?

2. In the 1992/1993 season, the runners-up suffered defeat against which club to hand the title to Manchester United?

3. Which player did Arthur Albiston replace to make his F.A cup debut for Manchester United in the 1977 victory against Liverpool?

4. Who's nickname was 'El Beatle'?

5. Where did Manchester United sign Roy Keane from?

6. Which club did Andrei Kanchelskis join upon leaving Manchester United?

7. In the 1985 FA Cup Semi-Final replay Manchester United defeated Liverpool 2-1. Which two players scored Manchester United's goals?

8. Which Manchester United player scored against the same goalkeeper for three different teams in 1963?

9. Who were Manchester United's opponents in the European Cup-Winners Cup semi-final in 1991?

10. What club did Manchester United re-sign Cristiano Ronaldo from in 2021?

11. Which team did Brian McClair join from?

12. What was Manchester United's first loss of the 2019-20 season in the Premier League?

13. In 1993, under Sir Alex Ferguson, Manchester United became English league champions for the first time in how many years?

14. Denis Law has enjoyed a number of hat-tricks as a Manchester United player. Against how many different teams did he score a hat-trick?

15. Manchester United's most successful manager, Sir Alex Ferguson, used to be the manager of which Scottish club?

16. After the 2006 World Cup, how many World Cup winners had played for Manchester United?

17. Which player failed to attend a drug test in 2003, receiving a large fine and an eight month ban?

18. From which club was Eric Cantona signed?

19. George Best had 470 appearances for Manchester United. Where was he from?

20. Which Spanish team knocked Manchester United out of the European Champions League in April 2000?

Answers:

1. Second

2. Oldham Athletic

3. Stewart Houston

4. George Best

5. Nottingham Forest

6. Everton

7. Robson and Hughes

8. Denis Law

9. Legia Warsaw

10. Juventus

11. Celtic

12. Crystal Palace, at home

13. 26

14. 16

15. Aberdeen

16. 6

17. Rio Ferdinand

18. Leeds United

19. Northern Ireland

20. Real Madrid

# # #

Round 6:

1. Why was Rio Ferdinand banned for eight months in January 2004?

2. Where was George Best born?

3. In the 1992-1993 season, Manchester United had a crucial game against Sheffield Wednesday at Old Trafford. Manchester United won with two headed goals scored in injury time by Steve Bruce. Who supplied the cross which led to Bruce's second goal?

4. During the 1981-1982 season, Manchester United had two players who played in every game. Who were they?

5. At what ground did Dwight Yorke make his debut for Manchester United?

6. Brian McClair also had a nickname. What was it?

7. Where did Manchester United sign Frank Stapleton from?

8. How many times did Manchester United win the FA Cup during the 1990s?

9. Which defender scored a very rare goal to help Man Utd reach the European Cup Final in 1968, at the semi final stage?

10. What was the shirt most often worn by George Best during his career at Manchester United?

11. Who scored the winning goal for Manchester United in the 1999 Champions League final?

12. In what year was the Munich air crash?

13. What colours did Manchester United play in, home, away,

and third, respectively?

14. Who used the number 8 jersey in the 2004-2005 season for Manchester United?

15. Carlos Tevez scored one hat-trick at Manchester United, when he scored four goals in one match against this team. His record against this team is five goals in five appearances. Which team?

16. At the time of the Munich Air Disaster in February 1958, who was the Manchester United manager?

17. Who were Manchester United's last European opponents before the English ban was placed?

18. Which former manager resigned from his job with ITV, after making a racist comment live on air about Marcel Desailly in April 2004?

19. From which Russian club was Ukrainian Andrei Kanchelskis signed?

20. Who was the first Manchester United manager from outside of England?

Answers:

1. Because he missed a routine drug test

2. Belfast

3. Gary Pallister

4. Albiston & Wilkins

5. Upton Park

6. Choccy

7. Arsenal

8. 4

9. William Foulkes

10. 7

11. Ole Gunnar Solskjaer

12. 1958

13. Red, Beige, and Black

14. Wayne Rooney

15. Blackburn Rovers

16. Matt Busby

17. Videoton

18. Ron Atkinson

19. Shakhtar Donetsk

20. Scott Duncan

# # #

Round 7:

1. Which Manchester United footballer played for England no less than 106 times, and scored 49 goals?

2. In the 1999 Champions League final, Manchester United scored two late goals to win the title. Who were the scorers?

3. Against which club did Mark Hughes get his first senior hat trick for Manchester United?

4. During the 1974-75 season, which team did Manchester United draw 2-2 against to confirm their second division championship and promotion back to the top flight?

5. Manchester United reshuffled their coaching staff in 2002. Can you name the coach brought in to look after the under 17s academy side?

6. In the 1998-1999 Champions League Final v Bayern Munich, Solskjaer and Sheringham came on as substitutes. Which two players did they replace?

7. Who's nickname was 'Jaws'?

8. Where did Manchester United sign Bryan Robson from?

9. When Andy Cole signed from Newcastle United, who went the other way as part of the deal?

10. Who scored Manchester United's goal in the 1-0 victory over Liverpool in the 1979 FA Cup Semi-Final replay?

11. Who scored a hat trick against Manchester City in the 5-0 victory?

12. On 17th December 2000 Manchester United lost at home 0-1 to Liverpool. Who was the last team (before this loss) to beat

Manchester United at Old Trafford in a league game?

13. Who scored the winning goal in the 1990 F.A. Cup final?

14. Which player, after several successful seasons at Manchester United, left for Inter Milan in January 2020?

15. Following a 3-1 defeat in the opening game of the 1995-1996 league season, which TV football pundit famously said of Manchester United, and Sir Alex Ferguson, that "You win nothing with kids"?

16. Shinji Kagawa scored his first Manchester United hat-trick against Norwich City. When was this match and in what competition?

17. By what nickname were Manchester United known during the late 1950s?

18. Only one team scored six goals in a Premiership game against Utd in the 1990s. Who were they?

19. Which former Manchester United player had a liver transplant in 2002, yet continued to drink alcohol?

20. From which club was Danish Goalkeeper Peter Schmeichel signed?

Answers:

1. Bobby Charlton

2. Teddy Sheringham & Ole Gunnar Solskjaer

3. Aston Villa

4. Notts County

5. Francisco Filho

6. Jesper Blomqvist & Andy Cole

7. Joe Jordan

8. West Bromwich Albion

9. Keith Gillespie

10. Jimmy Greenhoff

11. Andrei Kanchelskis

12. Middlesbrough

13. Lee Martin

14. Ashley Young

15. Alan Hansen

16. March 2013, Premiership

17. The Busby Babes

18. Southampton

19. George Best

20. Brondby

# # #

Round 8:

1. What are the standard colours for Manchester United's home games?

2. Who was manager of Manchester United between 1946 and 1969?

3. Manchester United won the European Champions League in 1999. When was the previous time they had won it?

4. Who scored the only goal, as Liverpool inflicted Manchester United's first home Premiership defeat of the 2000-01 campaign?

5. During the 1955-1956 season: a win against which team was their game of the season?

6. Carlos Queiroz, the assistant manager for the 2002-2003 season, is from which country?

7. In September 1956, Manchester United beat Anderlecht 10-0 in what is a record win for the club. Which player scored four goals in that match?

8. Ray Wilkins. What was his nickname?

9. Where did Manchester United sign Denis Law from?

10. How many goals did Eric Cantona score for Manchester United?

11. Two years previous to the Semi-Final victory above, Manchester United met Liverpool in the FA Cup Final itself, and won. What was the score in the 1977 FA Cup final?

12. Who was the player 'responsible' for getting Paul Scholes booked in the semi-final against Juventus, thus robbing him of a

chance to play in the final?

13. What country is Quinton Fortune from?

14. Vodafone were Manchester United's first, second, or third sponsors?

15. Who scored two goals against Manchester United in 2019-2020, both home and away?

16. Perhaps Sir Alex Ferguson's greatest achievement at Manchester United was winning the treble of English Premiership, FA Cup and European Cup in 1999. Which of Manchester United's four recognised strikers did *NOT* score in either final, or the last day of the league season?

17. He was famously known as the Super Sub and on one occasion he came from the bench in the 72nd minute and scored four goals in twelve minutes. The player is Ole Gunnar Solskjaer - against which team did he score those four goals?

18. What is the name of Manchester United's training ground?

19. Who was Manchester United's first international signing?

20. Which manager was cleared of a traffic offence in 1999 after explaining he had severe diarrhoea and needed to reach a toilet, which was why he was driving on a motorway hard shoulder?

Answers:

1. Red jersey, white shorts and black socks

2. Sir Matt Busby

3. 1968

4. Danny Murphy

5. Portsmouth

6. Mozambique

7. Dennis Viollet

8. Butch

9. Torino

10. 80

11. 2-1

12. Didier Deschamps

13. South Africa

14. Second

15. Matty Longstaff

16. Dwight Yorke

17. Nottingham Forest

18. Carrington

19. Nikola Jovanovic

20. Sir Alex Ferguson

# # #

Round 9:

1. From which club was defender David May signed?

2. When did Manchester United win their first Premiership title?

3. Which was the first team to beat Manchester United in a European Cup or Champions League tie at Old Trafford?

4. Who was the Manchester United manager on a temporary basis after the departure of David Moyes in 2014

5. Which former Manchester United wing-half became a coach at Old Trafford, then lost his life at Munich?

6. 1994-95: in one of the closest ever finishes to a league season, Manchester United were pipped to the post by Blackburn Rovers. Which London team ultimately denied Manchester United on the final day of the season?

7. Peter Schmeichel joined arch-rivals Manchester City in 2002. Against which team did he score his only goal for Manchester United?

8. Manchester United were relegated in the 1973-1974 season after a humiliating defeat to Manchester City. Who were the other two teams relegated with Manchester United that year?

9. I was known as 'The Great Dane'. Who am I?

10. Where did Manchester United sign Jim Leighton from?

11. Which county cricket club did one time United man Arnie Sidebottom play for?

12. To reach that 1977 Cup Final, which team did Manchester United beat in the Semi-   Final?

13. The first Red Cafe, outside of Manchester, opened in mid-2000. Where?

14. Which club did Peter Schmeichel join when he left Manchester United?

15. Who were Manchester United's closest rivals in the race for the 1992-1993   championship?

16. Ole Gunnar Solskjaer said that someone would return to Old Trafford in the 2020-21 season and "prove the fans wrong". Who?

17. When Peter Schmeichel left Manchester United at the end of the 1998-99 season, who did Sir Alex Ferguson bring in as a replacement?

18. When did Manchester United win their first Premiership title?

19. Dimitar Berbatov scored a hat-trick against Liverpool in 2010. Before this match the last hat-trick to be scored in a match between the two teams was in 1946. Another player came close to another hat-trick in that same match (he scored two goals). Who was this player?

20. Which former Manchester United player was appointed captain of Newcastle United in the 2010-11 season?

Answers:

1. Blackburn Rovers

2. 1992-93

3. Fenerbahce

4. Ryan Giggs

5. Bert Whalley

6. West Ham United

7. Rotor Volgograd

8. Norwich City & Southampton

9. Peter Schmeichel

10. Aberdeen

11. Yorkshire

12. Leeds United

13. Dublin

14. Sporting Lisbon

15. Aston Villa

16. Alexis Sanchez

17. Mark Bosnich

18. 1992-1993

19. Steven Gerrard

20. Alan Smith

# # #

Round 10:

1. What was significant about Pat McGibbon's debut in a League Cup tie in 1995?

2. Which former Manchester United player was exposed as having an affair with Sky Sports reporter Claire Tomlinson in 2000?

3. From which club was striker Ole Gunnar Solskjaer signed?

4. What do Cristiano Ronaldo, Eric Cantona, Andrei Kanchelskis, and Juan Sebastian Veron have in common?

5. What were Manchester United originally called when they were first created?

6. Of the survivors of the Munich air crash, two players never played again. One was an England winger. What was his name?

7. In the last game of the 1994-1995 season against West Ham United, which West Ham player put Manchester United 1-0 behind?

8. In the 1993-1994 season, Eric Cantona was sent off in two successive games for Manchester United. Who were the opposition?

9. Who was known as 'Big Norm'?

10. Where did Manchester United sign Henning Berg from?

11. In the 1963 FA Cup Semi-Final, Manchester United defeated Southampton 1-0 en route to their third FA Cup Final victory. Who scored the only goal of the game?

12. Who scored the winning goal in Manchester United's first League Cup triumph?

13. How many points did Manchester United win the league by in season 1999-2000?

14. What was Ryan Giggs's name when he was born?

15. Why was Manchester United's victory at Carrow Road in 2020 disappointing?

16. In 2001, Jaap Stam was allowed to leave Manchester United, a move which Sir Alex Ferguson would later refer to as his biggest mistake. Which Italian club did Stam move to?

17. Who scored Manchester United's goal in the Champions League Final in 2008?

18. The date was 28th August 2011 and the final result was 8-2. Wayne Rooney scored his sixth hat-trick for club. Which team were Manchester United playing against?

19. In January 1995, Eric Cantona was banned from playing professional football for eight months after doing what to a Crystal Palace fan at the end of a match?

20. Bobby Charlton made his final league appearance for Manchester United in 1973, but his day was spoilt by a 1-0 defeat at which ground?

Answers:

1. He was sent off and never played for Manchester United again

2. Bryan Robson

3. Molde

4. First players to play for United from their respective countries

5. Newton Heath

6. Johnny Berry

7. Michael Hughes

8. Swindon Town & Arsenal

9. Norman Whiteside

10. Blackburn Rovers

11. Denis Law

12. Brian McClair

13. 18

14. Ryan Wilson

15. Marcus Rashford and Anthony Martial both missed penalties.

16. Lazio

17. Cristiano Ronaldo

18. Arsenal

19. Karate-kicking him

20. Stamford Bridge

# # #

Round 11:

1. Most remember the 9-0 rout of Ipswich Town and Andy Cole's five goal haul in 1995, but who opened the scoring that day?

2. Sir Alex Ferguson is known for his bad temper and in 2003 during one of his 'hissy fits' kicked a boot, which hit a player and cut him above his eye. The cut required stitches. Who was the player?

3. From which Midlands club was Dwight Yorke signed?

4. When did the Munich Air Disaster happen?

5. Which club signed Andy Cole from Manchester United in 2001?

6. Which number are David Beckham, Eric Cantona, Bryan Robson, and George Best, all famous for wearing with Manchester United?

7. Which Liverpool player once attempted to upset Eric Cantona, by turning down his collar?

8. 1995-96: another last day decider. At which ground did Manchester United travel to and record a 3-0 win, to win the title?

9. On 5th May 1999, Manchester United travelled to Anfield and took a 2-0 lead through Dwight Yorke, and a Denis Irwin penalty, but they were pegged back to 2-2 after a last-minute Paul Ince equaliser. What significance would this match have on United's season?

10. 'Dolly and Daisy'. One was Gary Pallister, who was the other?

11. Where did Manchester United sign Mickael Silvestre from?

12. Who scored Manchester United's winning goal in the 1996 FA Cup Final against Liverpool?

13. What was the first ever number worn by Eric Cantona for Manchester United?

14. Who scored the goal which is said to have saved Sir Alex Ferguson's job as manager of Manchester United?

15. Where did Manchester United sign Dennis Irwin from?

16. Which young prospect became the heart and soul of Manchester United's first team's right wing in 2019-2020?

17. 1995-96 season: Manchester United won a crucial game against Leeds United at Old Trafford 1-0 but which Leeds player was forced to play in goal after the keeper, Mark Beeney, was sent-off early in the match?

18. Diego Forlan finally broke his duck for United with a penalty against Maccabi Haifa in what was his 27th appearance but one player had to wait until his 30th appearance for his first goal for Manchester United. Who was he?

19. Manchester United suffered a 3-1 defeat in the 1994 League Cup Final (Coca-Cola Cup) at the hands of Aston Villa. Which Manchester United Player was sent off for deliberate handball on the goal line in that match?

20. Which players were brought in during the 2019 summer to fill in as a centre back and right back, respectively?

Answers:

1. Roy Keane

2. David Beckham

3. Aston Villa

4. February 1958

5. Blackburn Rovers

6. 7

7. Neil Ruddock

8. The Riverside Stadium

9. Denis Irwin was sent-off and was banned for the FA Cup Final that year

10. Steve Bruce

11. Inter Milan

12. Eric Cantona

13. 12

14. Mark Robins

15. Oldham Athletic

16. Mason Greenwood

17. Lucas Radebe

18. Garry Birtles

19. Andrei Kanchelskis

20. Harry Maguire and Aaron Wan-Bissaka

# # #

Round 12:

1. In the treble winning season 1998-1999, Manchester United faced Tottenham Hotspur at Old Trafford knowing they needed a victory to be sure of beating Arsenal to the title, but who were main challengers Arsenal facing on the same day at Highbury?

2. What is the nationality of Gordon Strachan?

3. Which Manchester United player became the first ever player to be crowned PFA young player of the year in 1992?

4. Which Championship side did Daniel James represent before Manchester United bought him in 2019?

5. Sir Alex Ferguson guided Manchester United to their third European Cup/Champions League success, the second under his management, in 2008. Which team, from England, did they face in the final?

6. Who were the scorers in the 1998-1999 treble winning season's final league game against Tottenham Hotspur?

7. Who is the missing player: Charlton, Wilkins, Robson, Beckham and which one?

8. We all remember Ryan Giggs' goal against Arsenal in the semi-final replay of 1999, but that game should never have taken place after a "perfectly good goal" was disallowed in the first game. Who scored that disallowed goal?

9. Who did Mason Greenwood overcome as fastest individual sprinter during a game with his 37.6km/h sprint against Everton at Goodison Park?

10. In the 1997-1998 season, Arsenal claimed a heart-breaking victory at Old Trafford which went a long way to taking the title

to Highbury. Which Arsenal player scored the winning goal?

11. Former Manchester United winger Andrei Kanchelskis has a unique claim to fame. What is it?

12. In what year were the club now known as Manchester United formed?

13. Who was on the scoresheet against Linzer ASK in the March 2020 game behind closed doors; in scoring order?

14. Sir Alex Ferguson retired from management at the end of the 2012-2013 season, after 27 years in charge of Manchester United. Which team did Manchester United face in his last game in charge?

15. How many players scored against Bayern Munich in the 1998-1999 Champions League?

16. What do Denis Irwin, Roy Keane, Peter Schmeichel and Ryan Giggs all have in common?

17. Which playmakers did Manchester United have on their radar for the January 2021 window but did not buy?

18. Which prolific Manchester City winger did Aaron Wan-Bissaka "keep in his pocket" both home and away in 2019-2020?

19. Who helped Bruno Fernandes settle in the most at Manchester United in 2019-20?

20. Which player had an injury-prone season in 2019/2020?

Answers:

1. Aston Villa

2. Scottish

3. Ryan Giggs

4. Swansea City

5. Chelsea

6. Manchester United 2 (Beckham, Cole) Tottenham 1 (Ferdinand)

7. Paul Ince

8. Roy Keane

9. Fred (Frederico Rodrigues de Paula Santos)

10. Marc Overmars

11. Played in the Manchester, Merseyside and Old Firm Derbies

12. 1878

13. Ighalo, James, Mata, Greenwood, and Pereira

14. West Bromwich Albion

15. 5

16. All won 3 domestic doubles during the 1990s

17. Jack Grealish and James Maddison

18. Raheem Sterling

19. Diogo Dalot

20. Paul Pogba

# # #

Round 13:

1. What was Manchester United's record in the Premier League when the season was postponed in March 2020? (W-D-L)

2. What position did Andreas Pereira mainly operate in before the announcement of Manchester United's biggest January 2020 signing?

3. Which feat did Ole Gunnar Solskjaer and Nuno Esperito Santo both achieve in the 2019/2020 season which only Antonio Conte had previously achieved?

4. Until Watford's display on February 29, what feat did only Manchester United achieve in the league?

5. What was Manchester United's last game before the season was postponed in March 2020?

6. Which player is affectionately known as 'The King' to Manchester United fans?

7. Which two players were suspended for Manchester United's 1999 Champions League final triumph?

8. Prior to wearing No. 7, David Beckham wore which number at Manchester United?

9. Who scored the winning goal for Manchester United in their 2-1 Champions League final victory in 1999?

10. Which player holds the distinction of being Manchester United's longest-serving captain?

11. Which player took the No. 7 jersey after Cristiano Ronaldo

left?

12. Sir Alex Ferguson famously kicked a boot at which player, injuring his eye?

13. Which Brazilian twin brothers played for Manchester United?

14. Louis van Gaal mistakenly referred to which Manchester United player as 'Mike' in a press conference?

15. The players who progressed to the Manchester United first-team under Matt Busby were known as what?

16. Manchester United broke their record transfer fee in 2016 when they paid £89.5 million for which player?

17. As of 2020, Manchester United hold the record for most league titles in England. How many times have they been champions?

18. What is Manchester United's record win (all competitions)?

19. Which player holds the record for most Manchester United appearances?

20. At 46 years, 281 days, which player was the oldest to ever appear for Manchester United?

Answers:

1. 12-9-8

2. Central attacking midfielder

3. Defeated Pep Guardiola's Manchester City twice in the premier league

4. Took points off of Liverpool

5. LASK in the Europa League

6. Eric Cantona (Denis Law also acceptable)

7. Roy Keane and Paul Scholes

8. No. 10 and No. 24 (both answers acceptable)

9. Ole Gunnar Solskjaer

10. Bryan Robson (12 years)

11. Michael Owen

12. David Beckham

13. Rafael and Fabio

14. Chris Smalling

15. The Busby Babes

16. Paul Pogba

17. Twenty (20) times. (Most recent title was 2012-13)

18. 10-0 versus Anderlecht in the preliminary round of the 1956-57 European Cup

19. Ryan Giggs (with 963 appearances between 1991 and 2014)

20. Billy Meredith (against Derby County on May 7, 1921)

# # #

Round 14:

1. Manchester United's record Champions League win came in 2007 against Roma. What was the score?

2. Which player holds the record for most Manchester United goals?

3. With a reign of 26 years, 194 days, who is the longest-serving Manchester United manager?

4. The highest transfer fee ever received by Manchester United was £80 million in 2009 - for which player?

5. Manchester United inflicted their biggest Premier League win (9-0), on which opponent in 1995?

6. In what year was Old Trafford built?

7. Who were Manchester United's opponents in the first game at Old Trafford?

8. What is the capacity of Old Trafford (as of 2020)?

9. What is the nickname of Old Trafford?

10. Two stands at Old Trafford are named after which people?

11. The West Stand of Old Trafford is more famously known as what?

12. A statue called 'The United Trinity' stands outside Old Trafford, featuring which three players?

13. Old Trafford is situated on what road?

14. Manchester United played at which two grounds before moving to Old Trafford?

15. The 2003 Champions League final was held at Old Trafford. Which two teams played in it?

16. Which team knocked out Manchester United in the 1965/1966 European Cup?

17. Sir Alex Ferguson wanted Roy Keane to be Manchester United's number what, before David Beckham took it instead?

18. Who kicked a fan during a game for Manchester United?

19. Which Manchester United legend spent time with Manchester City as a schoolboy footballer?

20. The famous 'Dab' dance move was invented by which players?

Answers:

1. 7-1 (Man Utd's goals scored by: M. Carrick x2, W. Rooney, A. Smith, C. Ronaldo, R. Giggs and P. Evra).

2. Wayne Rooney (with 253 goals - Bobby Charlton is second with 249 goals).

3. Sir Alex Ferguson.

4. Cristiano Ronaldo (sold to Real Madrid).

5. Ipswich Town.

6. 1910.

7. Liverpool (February 19, 1910. Game finished Man Utd 3-4 Liverpool)

8. 74,000.

9. The Theatre of Dreams.

10. Sir Bobby Charlton and Sir Alex Ferguson.

11. The Stretford End.

12. George Best, Denis Law and Bobby Charlton.

13. Sir Matt Busby Way.

14. North Road and Bank Street.

15. Juventus and AC Milan.

16. Partizan

17. 7

18. Eric Cantona 'kung fu'

19. Ryan Giggs

20. Cam Newton

# # #

Round 15:

1. Manchester United once pulled out of the FA Cup in order to play in which   competition?

2. Irish golfer Rory McIlroy supports Manchester United and is friends with which club legend?

3. Sir Alex Ferguson did not win the league with Manchester United until his which season in charge?

4. Who is the only player to win the European Golden Boot while playing for Manchester United?

5. Before they became Manchester United, the club was known by what name?

6. In Manchester United's 2008 Champions League final victory over Chelsea on penalties, who was the only Red Devils player to miss a spot-kick?

7. Which team did Manchester United play in the game that became known as 'The Battle of the Buffet'?

8. Chesney Brown, a character in the British soap opera Coronation Street, had a Great Dane dog named after which Manchester United player?

9. What is the name of Manchester United's mascot?

10. Which Manchester United manager is said by fans to be "at the wheel"?

11. Who said: "When the seagulls follow the trawler, it's because they think sardines will be thrown into the sea"?

12. Which pundit, referring to Alex Ferguson's Manchester United team in 1995, famously said: "You can't win anything with kids"

13. Who was Sir Alex Ferguson's first signing as Manchester United manager?

14. How many league titles have Manchester United won?

15. Manchester United were formed as Newton Heath in which year?

16. Who did Wayne Rooney surpass to become Man Utd's all-time top scorer?

17. Who did Sir Alex Ferguson replace as United boss in 1986?

18. Which team did Manchester United beat to win the 1968 European Cup final?

19. Who scored Manchester United's two goals in the 1999 Champions League?

20. How much did Cristiano Ronaldo cost Manchester United in 2003?

Answers:

1. The Club World Cup

2. Sir Alex Ferguson

3. Seventh

4. Cristiano Ronaldo (31 goals in 2009).

5. Newton Heath.

6. Cristiano Ronaldo.

7. Arsenal.

8. Peter Schmeichel.

9. Fred the Red.

10. Ole Gunnar Solskjaer.

11. Eric Cantona.

12. Alan Hansen.

13. Viv Anderson.

14. 20

15. 1878

16. Sir Bobby Charlton

17. Ron Atkinson

18. Benfica

19. Solskjaer and Sheringham

20. £12 million

# # #

Round 16:

1. Who scored Manchester United's winning goal vs Liverpool in the 1996 FA Cup final?

2. Which player has made the most appearances for Manchester United?

3. Where did Manchester United lift the European Cup for the third time in 2008?

4. What year did the Glazer family complete their takeover of Manchester United?

5. Which player scored a hat-trick in Sir Alex Ferguson's final game?

6. Which two shirt numbers did David Beckham wear before No. 7?

7. Which player became Manchester United's No. 7 when Cristiano Ronaldo left in 2009?

8. Which two Premier League sides have Manchester United beaten 9-0?

9. Who replaced Roy Keane as Manchester United captain in 2005?

10. Who was the first player to win the Ballon d'Or while playing for Manchester United?

11. What is the colour of Manchester United's mascot?

12. Which of these has NOT won Manchester United's Player of the Year awards?

13. Who has won Manchester United's Player of the Year award the most times?

14. Which club did Wayne Rooney score a hat trick against on his

Manchester United debut?

15. Which Manchester United player scored an extra time goal to win the 2016 FA Cup final?

16. Which Manchester United player became the first ever to be sent off in an FA Cup Final?

17. Who scored Bayern Munich's goal in the 1999 European Cup Final?

18. A scout sent a telegram to a Manchester United manager saying 'I think I've found you a genius'. Which player was the scout referring to?

19. Three players who played in the same Manchester United team won European Footballer of the Year award, now the Ballon D'or. Name them.

20. Who is the oldest player to play for Manchester United in the post-war period?

Answers:

1. Eric Cantona

2. Ryan Giggs

3. Moscow

4. 2005

5. Romelu Lukaku

6. 10 and 24

7. Michael Owen

8. Ipswich Town and Southampton

9. Gary Neville

10. Denis Law

11. Red

12. Peter Schmeichel

13. David De Gea

14. Fenerbache

15. Jesse Lingard

16. Kevin Moran

17. Mario Basler

18. George Best

19. Denis Law, George Best, Bobby Charlton

20. Edwin van der Sar (aged 40 in 2011)

# # #

Round 17:

1. Against which team did George Best scored six goals in 1970?

2. From which team did Manchester United purchase Fred in 2018?

3. In what year did Manchester United purchase Cristiano Ronaldo from Sporting Lisbon?

4. Against which team did Manchester United record their highest ever Premier League win, defeating them 9-0?

5. Which team did Peter Schmiechel join Manchester United from? And which team did he leave Old Trafford for?

6. Who was Sir Alex Ferguson's signing as Manchester United manager?

7. Sir Matt Busby stepped down as Manchester United manager in 1969. Who replaced him?

8. Which player did Sir Alex Ferguson once admit was his worst ever purchase as Manchester United manager?

9. Which Manchester United player won the English Footballer of the Year and PFA Player of the Year awards in 2000?

10. Which team ended Manchester United's European Cup campaign at the semi final stage in 1998?

11. Which Manchester United player missed their penalty in the Champions League final shoot-out in 2008 which United ultimately won against Chelsea?

12. Which team did Manchester United sign Steve Bruce from?

13. Since the 1980s, which Manchester United players have been full time captains England? There are four.

14. Manchester United legend Sir Matt Busby served most of his

playing career with which English club?

15. The 'United Trinity' refers to which trio of Manchester United players, as featured in a statue outside Old Trafford?

16. Who netted United's first-ever Premier League goal?

17. How many Manchester United players were in England's Euro 2016 squad? And can you name them?

18. Who was the captain of Manchester United in the inaugural 1992/93 Premiership season?

19. Which former Manchester United player had the nickname 'Chicharito' on his shirt? And what's the translation?

20. Eric Cantona scored the first hat-trick in the Premier League; how many hat-tricks did he score for Manchester United in the Premier League in total?

Answers:

1. Northampton Town

2. Shakthar Donetsk

3. 2003

4. Ipswich Town

5. Brondby, Sporting Lisbon

6. Viv Anderson

7. Wilf McGuinness

8. Ralph Milne

9. Roy Keane

10. Borussia Dortmund

11. Cristiano Ronaldo

12. Norwich City

13. Wayne Rooney, Rio Ferdinand, David Beckham, Bryan Robson

14. Manchester City (with 204 appearances)

15. George Best, Denis Law, and Sir Bobby Charlton

16. Mark Hughes

17. Three. Chris Smalling, Marcus Rashford, and Wayne Rooney

18. Bryan Robson

19. Hernandez. It means little pea.

20. None (he scored the first hat-trick playing for Leeds United)

# # #

Round 18:

1. Which former Manchester United favourite managed a Welsh club in 2014?

2. Who made 206 consecutive league appearances between 1977 and 1981?

3. Who comes third in the list of most appearances after Ryan Giggs and Sir Bobby Charlton?

4. Who scored four goals in 13 minutes against Nottingham Forest in the Premier League in 1999?

5. Which manager gave Dennis Law a free transfer in the summer of 1973 (after 11 years at the club)? And where did Law go?

6. Which player reached the milestone of 100 appearances for the club on 26 May 2021?

7. How many Premier League titles did Sir Alex Ferguson win with Manchester United?

8. Bryan Robson joined Manchester United in 1981 for a then record fee of £1.5 million from which club?

9. On the opening day of the 1996-97 season, David Beckham scored a goal from the halfway line to beat which club? And who was the unfortunate goalkeeper?

10. At which tournament was Cristiano Ronaldo involved in an incident where club teammate Wayne Rooney was sent off? (We need both the year and the tournament.)

11. Which player wore the number 7 shirt after Cristiano Ronaldo left?

12. Four players have won the Ballon d'Or while playing for

Manchester United, can you name them?

13. Which four members of the 1999 Treble-winning team made over 500 appearances for the club?

14. Who was the club's first non British and non Irish captain?

15. Three Scottish Internationals have played more than 450 times for the club, can you name them?

16. What was the club's original name before becoming Manchester United in 1902? And what were their original colours (two colours needed)?

17. Who were Manchester United's shirt sponsors from 1982 to 2000?

18. What is Sir Alex Ferguson's middle name?

19. In their first Premier League match Man Utd featured two foreign (not including Irish) players; name them.

20. In which year did Manchester United become the first English club to win the European Cup? And name both the successful manager and captain? Also, which club did they beat?

Answers:

1. Ole Gunnar Solskjær (the club was Cardiff City)

2. Steve Coppell

3. Paul Scholes

4. Ole Gunnar Solskjaer

5. Tommy Docherty, Manchester City

6. Aaron Wan-Bissaka

7. 13

8. West Bromwich Albion

9. Wimbledon. Neil Sullivan.

10. 2006 FIFA World Cup

11. Michael Owen

12. Denis Law (1964), Bobby Charlton (1966), George Best (1968), and Cristiano Ronaldo (2008)

13. Ryan Giggs, Denis Irwin, Gary Neville and Paul Scholes

14. Eric Cantona

15. Arthur Albiston (485), Brian McClair (471) and Martin Buchan (456) (note: Dennis Law made 404 appearances and Lou Macari 401)

16. Newton Heath, green and yellow

17. Sharp

18. Chapman

19. Peter Schmeichel and Andre Kanchelskis

20. 1968, Sir Matt Busby, Bobby Charlton, Benfica (1-4)

# # #

Round 19:

1. Who scored in 10 consecutive Premiership matches from 22 March 2003 to 23 August 2003?

2. Shortly after his departure from the club, Eric Cantona became captain of which French national team?

3. In the 1990s Manchester United had four captains. Name them?

4. Which two Manchester United players were members of England's 1966 World Cup winning team?

5. Manchester United beat which team 8-2 in the 2011/12 Premiership season?

6. Four Manchester United players have won European Footballer of the Year; name them?

7. In December 1998, which assistant coach left to become the manager of Blackburn Rovers?

8. Roy Keane had an infamous clash with Patrick Vieira in the Highbury tunnel and accused the Arsenal skipper of picking on which player?

9. Which former player broke Pele's record as the youngest player to appear in a World Cup?

10. What happened to Manchester United just six seasons after winning the European Cup?

11. The club has its training ground and academy headquarters near which village?

12. Which England international spent eleven years at Old Trafford, chiefly as Alex Stepney's understudy?

13. Who succeeded Tommy Docherty as manager in the middle of 1977?

14. As of 2021, who is the oldest player to win the Premier League?

15. Who scored two injury time goals to win the 1999 UEFA Champions League Final? And which team did Manchester United beat?

16. Who is Manchester United's CEO?

17. Which Manchester United footballer has the longest goal streak in the Premier League?

18. The most expensive transfer in Manchester United history?

19. Who is the top scorer in Manchester United history?

20. Which company is the technical sponsor of Manchester United?

Answers:

1. Ruud van Nistelrooy

2. French national beach football team

3. Bryan Robson, Steve Bruce, Eric Cantona and Roy Keane

4. Bobby Charlton and Nobby Stiles

5. Arsenal

6. Dennis Law (1964), Bobby Charlton (1966), George Best (1968), and Cristiano Ronaldo (2008)

7. Brian Kidd

8. Gary Neville

9. Norman Whiteside

10. They were relegated (in 1974 they became a Second Division club for the first time since 1938)

11. Carrington

12. Jimmy Rimmer

13. Dave Sexton

14. Edwin van der Sar (in 2011 at the age of 40 years and 205 days)

15. Teddy Sheringham. Bayern Munich.

16. Ed Woodward

17. Cristiano Ronaldo

18. Paul Pogba

19. Wayne Rooney

20. Adidas

# # #

Round 20:

1. How many times have Manchester United won the Champions League?

2. Which company is Manchester United's title sponsor?

3. In what year did Sir Alex Ferguson leave Manchester United?

4. When was the last time Manchester United became Premier League champion?

5. Who is the current captain of Manchester United in 2021?

6. Which Manchester United player won the Euros with his home nation?

7. How many spectators can Old Trafford Stadium hold?

8. As of 2020, How many trophies have Manchester United won since Sir Alex Ferguson left?

9. How many times have Manchester United players won the Golden Boot?

10. The most expensive sale in Manchester United history?

11. How many times have Manchester United players won the Ballon d'Or?

12. Which of the following players didn't win the World Cup as an Manchester United player?

13. As of October 2021, who is the most expensive player of the current Manchester United?

14. The youngest goalscorer in Manchester United's Premier League

history?

15. Who is Manchester United's record holder for matches played?

16. Who is Manchester United's biggest rival?

17. Who became Manchester United coach after Sir Alex Ferguson?

18. How many times has Manchester United won the Premier League?

19. In what year did Sir Alex Ferguson come to Manchester United?

20. As of October 2021, which eight players have made over 300 Premier League appearances for Manchester United?

Answers:

1. 3

2. Chevrolet

3. 2012

4. 2012-2013

5. David De Gea

6. Fabien Barthez

7. 75000

8. 4

9. 1

10. Romelu Lukaku

11. 4

12. Fabien Barthez

13. Bruno Fernandes

14. Federico Macheda

15. Ryan Giggs

16. Liverpool

17. David Moyes

18. 13

19. 1986

20.

a) Ryan Giggs (632)

b) Paul Scholes (499)

c) Gary Neville (400)

d) Wayne Rooney (393)

e) David De Gea (329)

f) Roy Keane (326)

g) Michael Carrick (316)

h) Rio Ferdinand (312)

# # #

Round 21:

1. Which four foreign countries have hosted Manchester United v Tottenham Hotspur matches?

2. Which eleven dutchmen played premier league football for Manchester United?

3. Which six players scored 10 or more goals for England while with Manchester United?

4. Who was the last player to be directly transferred between Manchester United & Liverpool FC?

5. Which six players scored 90 or more premier league goals for Manchester United?

6. Which five Italians played for Manchester United in the premier league?

7. Which six players have worn Manchester United's number five shirt in the premier league era?

8. Which eight Englishmen have won Manchester United's player of the year award between 1988 and 2019?

9. Who are the six goalkeepers that have worn Manchester United's number one shirt in the premier league era?

10. Who are the five players that scored UEFA Champions League hat-tricks for Manchester United?

11. Who are the four Scotsmen that have played for both Arsenal FC and Manchester United?

12. Who are the four players that scored Premier League hat-tricks against Manchester United?

13. Which five sponsors have appeared on Manchester United's Premier League shirts?

14. Where was Manchester United's first home UEFA European Cup game played?

15. Who are the six Brazilians that have played for Manchester United in the premier league?

16. Who had more than 60 premier league goals for Manchester United?

17. Who was Manchester United's top scorer in the 2009/2010 season?

18. Manchester United signed Bebe ahead of the 2009/2010 season. True or False?

19. Michael Owen scored the winner against Manchester City at Old Trafford in the 2009/2010 season. But who scored twice in the game?

20. Who scored the goal to knock Manchester United out of Europe that season?

Answers:

1. Canada (1952 Spurs 5-0 United), United States (1952 Spurs 7-1 United), Swaziland (1983 Spurs 1-2 United & Spurs 2-0 United) and China (2019 Spurs 1-2 United).

2. Daley Blind, Alexander Büttner, Tahith Chong, Jordi Cruyff, Memphis Depay, Timothy Fosu-Mensah, Raimond van der Gouw, Ruud van Nistelrooy, Robin van Persie, Edwin van der Sar and Jaap Stam.

3. Bobby Charlton(49), Wayne Rooney (44), Bryan Robson (25), Tommy Taylor (16), Paul Scholes (14) and David Beckham (11).

4. Phil Chisnall

5. Wayne Rooney (183 Goals), Ryan Giggs (109 Goals), Paul Scholes (107 Goals), Ruud Van Nistelrooy (95 Goals), Andrew Cole (93 Goals) and Ole Gunnar Solskjaer (91 Goals).

6. Matteo Darmian, Federico Macheda, Rodrigo Possebon, Giuseppe Rossi and Massimo Taibi.

7. Lee Sharpe (1993-96), Ronny Johnsen (1997-2002), Laurent Blanc (2002-03), Rio Ferdinand (2003-14), Marcos Rojo (2014-18) and Harry Maguire (2019-20).

8. Bryan Robson (1989), Gary Pallister (1990), Paul Ince (1993), David Beckham (1997), Teddy Sheringham (2001), Wayne Rooney (2006 & 2010), Michael Carrick (2013) and Luke Shaw (2019).

9. Peter Schmeichel (1993-99), Mark Bosnich (1999-2000), Fabien Barthez (2000-03), Tim Howard (2004-06), Edwin van der Sar (2006-11) and David De Gea (2011-2020).

10. Andy Cole (v Feyenoord & v Anderlecht), Wayne Rooney (v Fenerbahçe), Ruud   Van Nistelrooy (v Sparta Prague), Michael Owen (v Wolfsburg), Robin van Persie (v Olympiacos).

11. David Herd, Ian Ure, George Graham and Jim Leighton.

12. David Bentley (Blackburn Rovers), Dirk Kuyt (Liverpool), Romelu Lukaku (West Bromwich Albion) and Samuel Eto'o (Chelsea).

13. Sharp (1992-2000), Vodafone (2000-2006), AIG (2006-2010), Aon (2010-2014) and Chevrolet (2014-2020).

14. Maine Road against Anderlecht in October 1956. Old Trafford had yet to be fitted with floodlights.

15. Anderson, Fábio, Kléberson, Andreas Pereira, Rafael and Fred.

16.

    1) Wayne Rooney (183)

    2) Ryan Giggs (109)

    3) Paul Scholes (107)

    4) Ruud Van Nistelrooy (95)

    5) Andrew Cole (93)

    6) Ole Gunnar Solskjær (91)

    7) Cristiano Ronaldo (84)

    8) Eric Cantona (64)

    9) David Beckham (62

17. Wayne Rooney

18. False

19. Darren Fletcher

20. Arjen Robben

# # #

Round 22:

1. Gary Neville retired during the 2010/11 season. Who did he play his last game against?

2. Which club did Dimitar Berbatov score five goals against in one game?

3. Which Manchester United legend was Phil Jones compared to after his first few games for the club in the 2011/2012 season?

4. Which player did NOT start in central midfield when Manchester United beat Arsenal 8-2 in August 2011?

5. Which of these players made a first-team appearance for Manchester United during the 2011/2012 season?

6. Who did Sir Alex Ferguson dismiss as a "Television critic" when Manchester United were knocked out of the Champions League that season?

7. Paul Scholes wore number 22 on his return. Who inherited his old number 18 squad number?

8. Who did Robin van Persie score a hat-trick against to seal Manchester United's 20th league title?

9. Who scored Manchester United's last goal at Old Trafford under Sir Alex   Ferguson?

10. Which club did David Moyes say Manchester United need to be more like?

11. What food did David Moyes ban?

12. Who was Manchester United most expensive signing

during the 2013/2014 season?

13. Who played the fewest games for Manchester United during the 2014/2015 season?

14. Who did Wayne Rooney score his last goal for Manchester United against?

15. What is the nick name of Manchester United?

16. When did Manchester United adopt their current name?

17. Which English club has won the most trophies?

18. How many league titles have Manchester United won, as of 2021?

19. How many FA cups have Manchester United won, as of 2021?

20. How many FA Community Shields have Manchester United won, as of 2021?

Answers:

1. West Bromwich Albion

2. Blackburn Rovers

3. Ducan Edwards

4. Michael Carrick

5. Paul Pogba

6. Roy Keane

7. Ashley Young

8. Aston Villa

9. Rio Ferdinand

10. Manchester City

11. Oven chips

12. Juan Mata

13. Radamel Falcao

14. Tottenham Hotspur

15. Red Devils

16. 1902

17. Manchester United

18. 20

19. 5

20. 21

# # #

Round 23:

1. Which former player broke Pele's record as the youngest player to appear in a World Cup?

2. What happened to Manchester United just six seasons after winning the 1968 European Cup?

3. Manchester United has its training ground and academy headquarters near which village?

4. Which England international spent eleven years at Old Trafford, chiefly as Alex Stepney's understudy?

5. Who succeeded Tommy Docherty as manager in the middle of 1977?

6. As of 2021, who is the oldest player to win the Premier League?

7. Who scored two injury time goals to win the 1999 UEFA Champions League Final? And which team did Manchester United beat?

8. Who made seven appearances on loan for Manchester United in 2007?

9. Who took early retirement in 2004 having only made nine appearances for Manchester United over seven years?

10. Who made his club debut in the 2013 Community Shield?

11. Where is Bebe from?

12. Federico Macheda burst onto the scene against Aston Villa in 2009, what was the final score of that match?

13. Which striker had to wait over 20 games for his first goal for Manchester United?

14. Which player left Manchester United in 2000 to join Blackburn Rovers?

15. Which French player made his debut for Manchester United in the 2006/2007 season?

16. Which French goalkeeper played for Manchester United?

17. Who scored the first goal of the Sir Alex Ferguson era?

18. From which club did Manchester United sign legend Steve Bruce?

19. Who was Manchester United's first shirt sponsor?

20. Who was the first Manchester United player to score a European Cup hat-trick?

Answers:

1. Norman Whiteside

2. They were relegated (in 1974 they became a Second Division club for the first time since 1938)

3. Carrington

4. Jimmy Rimmer

5. Dave Sexton

6. Edwin van der Sar (in 2011 at the age of 40 years and 205 days)

7. Teddy Sheringham. Bayern Munich.

8. Henrik Larson

9. Michael Clegg

10. Wilfried Zaha

11. Portugal

12. 3-2

13. Diego Fortan

14. John Curtis

15. Patrice Evra

16. Fabien Barthez

17. John Sivebaek

18. Norwich City

19. Sharp

20. Tommy Taylor

# # #

Round 24:

1. From which club did Manchester United sign Javier Hernandez?

2. Which was the last English team Manchester United played before the Munich air disaster?

3. Which squad number did Andrei Kanchelskis end his Manchester United career with?

4. At the start of the 2010-2011 season how many (current) United players have captained their country on at least one occasion?

5. As of 2021, how many European semi-finals have Manchester United been knocked out of?

6. When Manchester United signed Andy Cole from Newcastle United, which Manchester United player went to Newcastle as part of the deal?

7. Manchester United's mascot is known as _____ The Red?

8. Who is the oldest player to have played for Manchester United?

9. In which years have Manchester United won a European trophy?

10. Who was the first Manchester United player to win BBC Sports Personality of the year?

11. In which country was Ryan Giggs born?

12. Who was the first English club to play Manchester United in European football?

13. Who is the current manager of Manchester United?

14. Who is the current captain of Manchester United?

15. Which Welshman holds the record for most Manchester United appearances with 963?

16. Which Englishman is Manchester United's all-time record goalscorer with 253?

17. Which legendary Scottish manager guided Manchester United to 38 trophies during his 26-year tenure?

18. With which club does Manchester United contest the Manchester Derby?

19. Who is the most-decorated captain in Manchester United's history?

20. Who is the only Manchester United player to win the Ballon d'Or during the Premier League era?

Answers:

1. Chivas

2. Arsenal

3. 14

4. 13

5. 9

6. Keith Gillespie

7. Fred

8. Billly Meredith

9. 1991, 1999, 2009

10. David Beckham

11. Wales

12. Tottenham Hotspur

13. Ole Gunnar Solskjær

14. Harry Maguire

15. Ryan Giggs

16. Wayne Rooney

17. Sir Alex Ferguson

18. Manchester City

19. Roy Keane

20. Cristiano Ronaldo

# # #

Round 25:

1. Which Scotsman managed Manchester United from 1945 until 1969, and again from 1970-1971?

2. Which goalkeeper saved the decisive penalty as Manchester United defeated Chelsea in a shootout in the 2008 UEFA Champions League Final?

3. In December 1931, how much did James W. Gibson invest to take control of the club?

4. In which year did Manchester United become the first English team to compete in the European Cup?

5. What is Manchester United's biggest victory on record?

6. In 1968, Manchester United became the first English club to win the European Cup, with a team that contained how many European footballers of the year?

7. Who was appointed Manchester United manager in June 1971?

8. Who did Dave Sexton replace as manager in 1977?

9. Who did Manchester United lose the 1979 FA Cup final to?

10. Under the management of Ron Atkinson, what competition did Manchester United win in 1983 and 1985?

11. Who did Manchester United beat to win the 1983 Charity Shield?

12. Who did Manchester United beat to win the 1982 League Cup?

13. Manchester United became the first English club to do the

Double twice when they won both competitions in which year?

14. Who did Manchester United beat to become the only British club to win the   Intercontinental Cup?

15. Who did Manchester United beat to win the 2004 FA Cup at the Millennium Stadium?

16. In the 2005–2006 season, Manchester United failed to qualify for which phase of the UEFA Champions League for the first time in over a decade?

17. In December 2008, the club became the first British team to win which international cup?

18. In 2010, Manchester United defeated which team 2–1 at Wembley to retain the League Cup?

19. Who took over as interim player-manager of Manchester United, on 22 April 2014?

20. When did Louis van Gaal replace David Moyes as Manchester United manager?

Answers:

1. Sir Matt Busby

2. Edwin Van Der Sar

3. £2,000

4. 1957

5. 10-0

6. Eight – Geoff Bent, Roger Byrne, Eddie Colman, Duncan Edwards, Mark Jones, David Pegg, Tommy Taylor and Billy Whelan.

7. Frank O'Farrell

8. Tommy Docherty

9. Arsenal

10. FA Cup

11. Liverpool

12. Nottingham Forest

13. 1995-1996

14. Palmeiros

15. Millwall

16. Knockout stages

17. FIFA Club World Cup

18. Aston Villa

19. Ryan Giggs

20. May 2014

# # #

Round 26

1. When did Malcolm Glazer die?

2. The FA Cup Manchester United won under Louis Van Gaal, was what number victory in this competition for the club?

3. Which former Porto, Chelsea, Inter Milan and Real Madrid manger was put in charge of Manchester United in May 2016?

4. José Mourinho guided the club to a 19th FA Cup Final, but they lost 1–0 to whom?

5. On 18 December 2018, Manchester United were in which place in the Premier League table?

6. What was the length of the contract given to Ole Gunnar Solskjaer when he was appointed manager of Manchester United?

7. Manchester United equalled the biggest win in Premier League history with how Many goals win against Southampton on 2 February 2021?

8. Where is Manchester United's club crest derived from?

9. What features heavily on Manchester United's club crest?

10. At the end of which season did Louis Van Gall leave as manager of Manchester United?

11. Who has owned Manchester United since 2005?

12. Which organisation once valued Manchester United at £2.65 billion?

13. What is the highest number of goals that Manchester United has scored in a league season?

14. Who has scored the most hat tricks for Manchester United?

15. The Salvation" and "Elizabeth" are two films starring which former Manchester United football player?

16. Who scored the only goal for Chelsea in the 2017/2018 season FA cup finals against Manchester United?

17. What shirt number did Mason Greenwood wear for Manchester United in the 2021/2022 season?

18. What shirt number did Bruno Fernandes wear for Manchester United in the 2021/2022 season?

19. What shirt number did Harry Maguire wear for Manchester United in the 2021/2022 season?

20. What shirt number did Aaron Wan-Bissaka wear for Manchester United in the 2021/2022 season?

Answers:

1. 28 May 2014

2. 12

3. José Mourinho

4. Chelsea

5. Sixth

6. Three years

7. 9-0

8. Manchester city council coat of arms

9. Ship

10. 2015/2016

11. The Glazer Family

12. Forbes

13. 103

14. Denis Law

15. Eric Cantona

16. Eden Hazard

17. 11

18. 18

19. 5

20. 29

# # #

Round 27:

1. What club did Denis Irwin join Manchester United from?

2. Who did Ryan Giggs score his first Manchester United goal against?

3. Who did Eric Cantona join Manchester United from?

4. Who did Steve Bruce score two late headers against in April 1993 to set Manchester United on the way to the title?

5. Who was Roy Keane due to sign for before joining Manchester United?

6. Who hurt their arm fighting Turkish police in November 1993?

7. How many goals did Eric Cantona score in the 1994 FA Cup final against Chelsea?

8. Who did Eric Cantona make his comeback against in October 1995?

9. Who did Ole Gunnar Solskjaer score against on his Manchester United debut in August 1996?

10. How many goals did Teddy Sheringham score in the season Manchester United won the treble?

11. In what competition did Ryan Giggs score his most famous goal against Arsenal?

12. What club did Peter Schmeichel leave Manchester United for?

13. Who did Manchester United lose to on the opening day of the 2020/2021 campaign?

14. How many goals did Marcus Rashford score in the 2020/2021 season?

15. Who did Alex Telles make his Manchester United debut against?

16. How many games did Manchester United win during the 2020/2021 Premier League season?

17. Which club inflicted Manchester United's heaviest defeat during the 2020/2021 season?

18. Which team did Manchester United beat to reach the 2021 Europa League Final?

19. How many Premier League games did Harry Maguire play for Manchester United during the 2020/2021 campaign?

20. Who missed the decisive penalty in Manchester United's shoot-out defeat to Villarreal in the Europa League Final?

Answers:

1. Oldham Athletic

2. Manchester city

3. Leeds United

4. Sheffield Wednesday

5. Blackburn Rovers

6. Bryan Robson

7. 2

8. Liverpool

9. Blackburn Rovers

10. 5

11. FA Cup

12. Sporting Lisbon

13. Crystal Palace

14. 21

15. Paris St-Germain

16. 21

17. Tottenham Hotspur

18. AS Roma

19. 34

20. David De Gea

# # #

Round 28:

1. What did Arsenal, Leicester City, Manchester United and Tottenham Hotspur have in common during the 2020/2021 season?

2. After the war, the club received how much in compensation from the War Damage Commission?

3. While reconstruction took place, Manchester United played its "home" games at Manchester City's which ground?

4. The roofs of stadium old Trafford were supported by pillars that obstructed many fans' views, and they were eventually replaced with which structure?

5. The Stretford End was the last stand to receive a cantilevered roof, completed in time for which season?

6. First used on 25 March 1957 and costing £40,000, four what 180-foot (55 m) were erected, each housing 54 individual floodlights in old Trafford?

7. The Taylor Report's requirement for an all-seater stadium lowered capacity at Old Trafford to around 44,000 in which year?

8. In 1995, the North Stand was redeveloped into three tiers, restoring capacity for how many people in Old Trafford?

9. At the end of which season, second tiers were added to the

East and West Stands, raising capacity to around 67,000 in old Trafford?

10. Between July 2005 and May 2006, how many seats were added via second tiers in the north-west and north-east quadrants in old Trafford?

11. Part of the new seating was used for the first time on 26 March 2006, when an attendance of how many people became a new Premier League record in old Trafford?

12. How many seats were unoccupied when 76,098 spectators saw Manchester United beat Blackburn Rovers 4–1?

13. In 2009, reorganisation of the seating resulted in a reduction of capacity by which number to 75,957?

14. Manchester United has the which highest average attendance of European football clubs only behind Borussia Dortmund?

15. How many different countries have Manchester United Supporter Clubs?

16. Deloitte estimate that Manchester United has how many fans worldwide?

17. How many Facebook followers does Manchester United have, as of July 2020?

18. Which study showed that Manchester United had the loudest fans in the Premier League?

19. Supporters of Manchester United are represented by how many independent bodies?

20. Which is the West Stand of Old Trafford is the home end and the traditional source of the club's most vocal support?

Answers:

1. None of them played a game that kicked off at 3pm on a Saturday

2. £22,278.

3. Maine Road

4. Cantilevered

5. 1993–1994 season

6. Pylons

7. 1993

8. 55000

9. 1998-99

10. 6000

11. 69,070

12. 114 seats

13. 255

14. Second

15. 24

16. 75 million

17. 72 million

18. 2014

19. Two

20. Stretford End

# # #

Round 29:

1. Which four other clubs are Manchester United considered to have serious rivalries with?

2. The rivalry with Liverpool is rooted in competition between the cities during the which revolution when Manchester was famous for its textile industry?

3. The "Roses Rivalry" with Leeds United stems from which historical event?

4. Which company was the club's first shirt sponsor at the beginning of the 1982–1983 season?

5. What was the last season that Manchester United were sponsored by Sharp Electronics?

6. Who was next to sponsor Manchester United after Sharp Electronics?

7. For how many seasons were Manchester United sponsored by Vodafone?

8. Which company was the club's shirt sponsor at the beginning of the 2006–2007 season?

9. Manchester United announced their first training kit sponsor in which year?

10. The contract for the training kit sponsorship was then sold to which company in April 2013 for a deal worth £180 million over eight years, which also included purchasing the naming rights for the Trafford Training Centre?

11. When did Manchester United signed a seven-year deal with American automotive corporation General Motors?

12. At the start of 2015–16 season, who manufactured Manchester United's kit as part of a world-record 10-year deal worth a minimum of £750 million?

13. Which plumbing products manufacturer became the club's first sleeve sponsor ahead of the 2018–19 season?

14. With whom did Manchester United sign a five-year, £235m sponsorship deal ahead of the 2021–22 season?

15. In what year did Manchester United become a limited company?

16. When were Manchester United floated on the stock market?

17. In May 2005, who purchased the 28.7 per cent stake held by McManus and Magnier, thus acquiring a controlling interest through his investment vehicle Red Football Ltd in a highly leveraged takeover valuing the club at approximately £800 million?

18. When did the club announced a £660 million debt refinancing package, resulting in a 30 per cent reduction in annual interest payments to £62 million a year?

19. What was the extent of Manchester United's debt in January 2010?

20. Who was Manchester United's goalkeeping coach in the 2021/2022 season?

Answers:

1. Arsenal, Leeds United, Liverpool, and Manchester City

2. The Industrial Revolution

3. The War of the Roses

4. Sharp Electronics

5. 1999-2000 Season

6. Vodafone

7. Four years

8. AIG

9. 2011

10. AON

11. 2012

12. Adidas

13. Kohler

14. TeamViewer

15. 1892

16. 1991

17. Malcolm Glazer

18. July 2006

19. £716.5 million

20. Richard Hartis

# # #

Round 30:

1. Former Manchester United central defender Nemanja Vidic hails from which country?

2. Paul Pogba joined Manchester united from Juventus. Who did he leave to join Juventus in the first place?

3. Who did Raphael Varane play for before Manchester United?

4. Who did Ole Gunnar Solskjaer manage before Manchester United?

5. Manchester United central defender Victor Lindelof hails from which country?

6. Manchester United central defender Eric Bailly hails from which country?

7. Juan Mata joined Manchester United from which club?

8. Tom Heaton rejoined Manchester United from which club?

9. What position does Tom Heaton play in?

10. Manchester United defender Diogo Dalot hails from which country?

11. Manchester United defender Alex Telles hails from which country?

12. Who did Aaron Wan-Bissaka play for before Manchester United?

13. Who did Jadon Sancho play for before Manchester United?

14. Who did Cristiano Ronaldo leave to re-join Manchester United?

15. Former Manchester United manager David Moyes is best known for his time in charge of which club?

16. Who did Phil Jones play for before Manchester United?

17. Who did Fred play for before Manchester United?

18. Manchester United forward Anthony Martial hails from which country?

19. Who missed an injury time penalty against Aston Villa during the 2021/2022 season contributing to a defeat for Manchester United?

20. Manchester United forward Edinson Cavani hails from which country?

21. Which Serbian midfielder played for Manchester United during the 2021/2022 season?

Answers:

1. Serbia

2. Manchester United

3. Real Madrid

4. Molde

5. Sweden

6. Ivory Coast

7. Chelsea

8. Aston Villa

9. Goalkeeper

10. Portugal

11. Brazil

12. Crystal Palace

13. Borussia Dortmund

14. Juventus

15. Everton

16. Blackburn Rovers

17. Shakhtar Donetsk

18. France

19. Bruno Fernandes

20. Uruguay

21. Nemanja Matic

# # #

Thankyou for using this book, I hope you have enjoyed it.

If you have enjoyed the book, please leave a review wherever you bought it - this will help other United fans find and enjoy the book as much as you have!

# # #

Printed by Nevno Publishing, in the United Kingdom.

First printing, 2021.

Printed in Great Britain
by Amazon